an inspiring tale of adaptation
to a changing environment

Finch Discoveries

Story by Ginger Wallis
Illustrations by Bert Dodson

Dancing Journey Press
THETFORD CENTER | VERMONT

Text copyright © 2014 Ginger Wallis
Illustrations copyright © 2014 Bert Dodson
All rights reserved.

Design :: Jenna Dixon :: djinna.com

978-0-9847662-2-2 (print)
978-0-9847662-3-9 (ebook)

Wallis, Ginger.
   Finch discoveries : an inspiring tale of adaptation
      to a changing environment / by Ginger Wallis ;
      illustrated by Bert Dodson.
         pages   cm
   SUMMARY: Scientists share their methods and
      discoveries as they watch finches adapt to wet seasons,
      dry seasons, a severe drought, and eight months with
      intense rains.
         Audience: Ages 9-13.
         ISBN 9780984766222
         ISBN 9780984766239
         1. Finches--Galapagos Islands--Juvenile literature.
   2. Galapagos Islands--Juvenile literature. [1. Finches--
Galapagos Islands. 2. Galapagos Islands.]   I. Dodson,
Bert, illustrator. II. Title.
QL696.P246W35 2013   598.8'83
                  QBI13-600173

Library of Congress Control Number: 2013952944

Printed in the United States of America   4 3 2 1   14 15 16 17 18

This book is dedicated to all scientists who help us understand how living beings respond to changes in their environments and to Frank Wallis, my brother.

Author's Note

This story is based upon true events that occurred on Daphne Major Island in the Galapagos Archipelago during the 1970s and 1980s.

These events were studied by scientists Peter and Rosemary Grant and their colleagues during years of field research on the island.

In this book I imagine being a guest of the Grants and observing, participating, and learning about their discoveries. While my participation may be imaginary, the science is not: the story told here reflects what the Grants learned about one of the finch species of Daphne Major Island and, yes, the birds landed on their shoulders.

ARRIVAL

I can't believe how lucky I am to be on this expedition with Peter and Rosemary Grant. I am a teacher and my school district has given me a grant to be an assistant on this research project on Daphne Major Island. I love wild places — not that a middle school biology classroom can't be wild in its own way! The Grants plan to study the finches on this island for more than a decade.

First impression — everything on this remote tropical island is different from home — the sounds, the hot, muggy air, and blue-footed boobies. So far, we've lugged our food and supplies (three-months' worth) from our boat to our camp, including water barrels that weigh fifty pounds each, set up tents near the rim of the volcano, and organized a kitchen inside a shallow cave with a ceiling not much higher than I am tall. Whew. I'm exhausted.

Scratch...

...scratch

...scratch.

In a bird's nest, on a cactus, on a small island in the Pacific Ocean, an egg was wobbling slightly, and faint sounds were coming from inside.

The brown-speckled mother and black-feathered father cocked their heads and watched as a baby bird struggled to burst from the egg. Her head and feet shoved hard against the shell that surrounded her.

Push. Rest. Push. Rest. Crack!

Finally the shell gave way, and Adelita kicked the bottom off. Her neck wobbled as she chirped and fluttered her scrawny wings to get her parents' attention.

I'm hungry!

HOLDING A BIRD

Today Rosemary taught me how to hold a bird. You put your index and middle finger around its head, and then cup your other fingers loosely around its body so that the chest can move in and out easily.

The first one we took from the mist net seemed to give me a funny look, her eyes like shiny black beads.

When I held her this morning, her heart beat so fast. I wish I could've read her mind.

She is a medium ground finch and her scientific name is *Geospiza fortis*. As both names (*geo* = ground; *spiza* = finch) imply, she feeds mostly on the ground.

I realize I've been calling my first bird "she," though at this age you can't yet tell the sexes apart.

I love this close connection to another species. Occasionally a bird stays in my hand, free to go, yet lingering for a while. When it finally bolts, I sense its wildness. It vanishes instantly!

I am beginning to see one of the joys of being a field biologist.

Just two weeks after hatching, Adelita left the dome-shaped nest for good and flew for the first time. The wind brushed her feathers.

Whee!

There seemed to be more to this flying business than she had thought. As the ground rushed up to meet her, Adelita opened her wings, spread her tail feathers and leaned back. She hit the ground hard and toppled onto a patch of grass, just missing one of the spiky cactuses that dotted the open rocky landscape.

Oops.

Over the next two weeks, the little adventurer perfected her flying. Then one day . . . whoosh! Her flight stopped as her toes and wings caught in a net of soft threads.

One of the humans gently untangled her from the net, and cradled her securely in one hand.

THE SCIENTISTS' CODE

Peter and Rosemary hope to band and measure all of the finches on the island. They use a tool called a caliper to do the measuring. The beak depths, widths, and lengths vary a lot among these birds, and since birds use their beaks to feed, these differences might be important. Today Rosemary attached four bands to the bird I thought gave me a funny look earlier. One band was orange, one black, one green, and one aluminum. The aluminum one bore a number, 1362. The combination of colors identifies this bird. We'll be able to recognize her without catching her again.

The animals on the island seem amazingly unafraid, maybe because they have very few predators and humans don't live on the island. One finch even landed on Peter's camera!

Though Adelita sensed that the human meant no harm, she shut her eyes.

What is going on?

The woman brought a ruler alongside her folded wing to measure it. Then she lined the ruler up against the leg, big toe, and beak. The depth—height of the beak from top to bottom—was measured, as well as the beak's length and width. The woman carefully fitted two small bands around each of Adelita's legs, and squeezed them closed.

After only a few minutes, the woman opened her hand. Adelita flew off and landed on a nearby cactus. She twisted her neck and pecked at the colorful bands on her legs for quite awhile.

I wonder what this is about?

She preened her feathers back into place. The bands felt light and did not grip her legs. She took to the air. She had gotten hungry, but didn't see her parents.

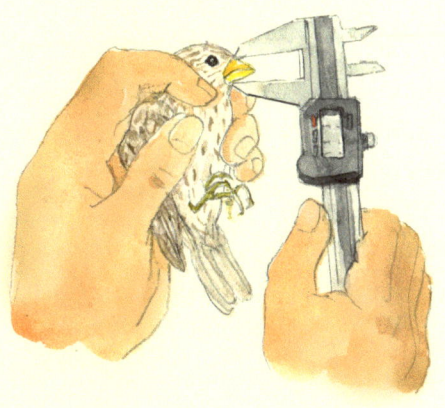

THE WET SEASON

Peter and Rosemary want to learn about the finches' food supply: what kinds of food they eat and how much of each kind. Part of their mission is to count every single seed on the plants and on the ground in areas called "plots." Can you imagine? Ninety of this kind, forty of that kind, on and on! They want to compare what the birds eat in the wet and dry seasons.

We've been observing the birds with binoculars, and Peter and Rosemary have already discovered something important. Despite the striking differences in the size and shape of their beaks, right now all the finches are feasting mostly on the same seven kinds of soft seeds!

Maybe the different beak shapes and sizes we measured don't really matter.

Adelita grew hungrier and hungrier. She spotted a young bird about her age pecking at a piece of bark on the ground.

Am I supposed to eat that?

She finally found her parents and studied what they were doing. Her father picked up a small grass seed with the tip of his beak and easily cracked it open.

Awkwardly, Adelita picked up a seed that looked similar.

Again and again, she clamped down hard with her beak.

Why are these seeds so tough?

She kept trying and finally . . . Snap! The shell broke open and she swallowed the delicious bits inside. The trick was using her tongue to push the seed to the back of her beak where the force was greatest.

Yummy! And I cracked it myself!

By the time Adelita was three months old, she really had the hang of feeding herself. Life was good! Early one morning she glanced up from feeding and turned her head. A short-eared owl on a rocky perch stared down at her.

Yikes.

Adelita took flight, looking for safety.

A cactus! I need a cactus. They have hiding places.

The landscape showed nothing but open space and two of those humans with strange equipment counting seeds on the ground.

The owl was gaining on her. Its sharp talons were ready to snatch her at any moment.

Adelita madly flapped her wings, veered sideways and down, and landed on the shoulder of one of the humans, the one who had given her the colorful leg bands. The owl swooped by.

That was too close for comfort!

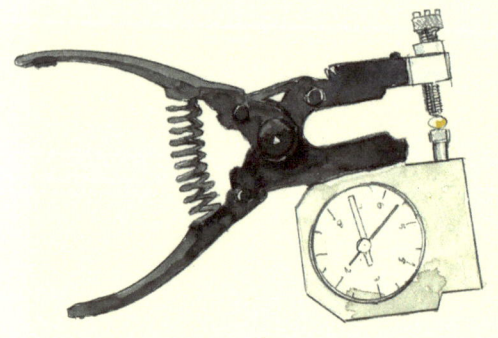

A CLEVER INVENTION

Yesterday a finch landed on my head, and today number 1362 landed on Rosemary's shoulder! We enjoy these friendly visits.

Peter has invented a new contraption—the McGill Nutcracker. It combines a pair of pliers with a scale that measures the force it takes to crack open an individual seed. With it, we've discovered that it takes twenty-four times more force to crack open the largest seeds than it does to crack open the smallest ones! Imagine the difference this makes to a bird. We've been on the island almost three months during the hot, wet season. Pretty soon Peter and Rosemary will go back to their university, and I'll return to my middle school students.

We'll come back in four months to see what things are like in the dry season. At least it will be cooler!

Four months later Adelita stood on top of a cactus and did not admire the view. The dry season had changed the island from green to brown. Many plants had dropped their leaves. Other plants had died. The only seeds left to eat had fallen to the ground.

Adelita breathed in the dry air. She flew down and pecked the thirsty ground, looking for a small, soft-shelled seed. She hopped about here and there, continuing the search.

Ah! There's one.

She grabbed it, but saw no others nearby. As each month went by, finding food became more difficult. It took more time and more energy.

What will tomorrow bring?

THE DRY SEASON

We arrive in August to find that the finches' beaks are a different color! They will turn black again next mating season.

The landscape looks dramatically different. No rain has fallen in April, May, June, or July. We see much more open rocky ground.

In our seed-counting plots we find fewer seeds on the ground and most of those look large and tough.

Thanks to the McGill Nutcracker, we can measure how tough.

These days the seeds are, on average, twelve times more difficult for the birds to crack than seeds during the wet season.

Will beak size be important in this dry period?

I've realized that to bring the island alive for my students, I need to take lots of photographs of the scientists working and of other animals in addition to the birds.

Besides, I can't resist the sea lions napping and the blue-footed boobies diving into the ocean for fish.

Adelita selected a large, tough fruit as long as her beak. It had long, pointed spines that stuck out in different directions. She closed her beak and tried to twist it.

This is a mouthful!

Over and over she shifted the spiny fruit to the base of her bill and brought it down with as much force as she could.

Why won't this crack?

She rested, her energy sapped. A big-beaked finch landed next to her. He picked up the same kind of fruit and cracked it open easily. He maneuvered the nutty, nutritious seeds from inside the fruit into his mouth and then flew away.

Show off. But look at him go!

She needed to find more food soon. She was still hungry.

CALTROP: HARD WORK!

This morning I accidentally stepped on a caltrop fruit.

Ouch! I could feel the sharp spine on the woody shell start to go into my bare foot. Its spines protected the seeds inside for sure!

I was amazed to learn from the Grants that a tiny difference in the depth of a finch's beak determines whether or not it can crack these fruits. A beak that can crack a caltrop can be only five millimeters thicker than a beak that's too small to be able to crack one. Five millimeters is about the thickness of five pieces of paper!

Peter and Rosemary have noticed that the finches are adjusting to the dry season by choosing the best seeds for their beak sizes and shapes. All finches are choosing the largest seeds they can crack to get the most energy for their efforts.

We're heading home now that the dry season is over. I can't come back next year, and I'm going to miss this place a lot. Maybe I'll come back in the future.

Adelita managed to find enough food to grow big and strong. At four years old, she had grown used to the annual wet and dry seasons and to the coming and going of the humans. But now something was wrong.

Why won't this dry season go away?

Her shiny black eyes scanned the ground. There were plenty of large, spiny fruits and some hard cactus seeds, but almost no small seeds.

A bird could starve around here.

Adelita's whole body felt the stress of hunger. Her feathers were damaged, and that was normal, but without enough food she didn't have the energy she needed to grow new ones. Distracted and worried, she lifted herself off the parched ground and flew.

Whoosh.

Once again her toes and wings caught in a pocket of soft threads. From past experience she knew that the humans would free her again. She could continue to look for food soon.

NUMBER 1362

Scientists have been coming to the island every year, but it has been four years since I've been back. Things look bleak.

My seed-counting plot has about half the number of seeds that I found before the drought.

We have found 150 dead finches. They look like little broken toys discarded on the ground.

The scientists have been catching and weighing the survivors. Number 1362, like many others, has lost one quarter of her weight.

I badly want to bring seeds from somewhere else to help the birds, but we're here to observe what happens naturally.

I watch the small-beaked birds struggle to survive, my heart breaking.

Adelita had an idea. Bracing her head against the rough surface of a rock, she tried to shove a smaller rock away with her feet. She worked hard, like a tiny, feathered bulldozer. She was weak from hunger, and neither rock budged.

I'll rest and try again.

A small, speckled lava lizard, well camouflaged, studied Adelita's efforts from inside a shady cave.

Push. Push.

Success! The smaller rock rolled away. Three little seeds were hidden underneath. Adelita gobbled them down, but her belly still grumbled. The lava lizard started to scuttle away. Adelita flew at it, swooped down and grabbed it in her beak.

What happened to the rest of it?

She held the wiggling tail in her beak and the lizard made its escape. She swallowed the tail.

A new food source!

Later, she noticed that other birds had also become creative with their food choices. One fellow finch had dined on a broken booby eggshell and another on blue-footed booby droppings.

I know I need to eat whatever I can find, but please, please rain soon because I am still a seedeater!

POPULATION DROP

The finches help themselves in marvelous ways in these tough times. We've seen new behaviors such as rolling rocks away to search every inch of ground and scavenging scraps from owl kills.

Still, birds continue to die. Before this long drought we counted 600 males and the same number of females.

Now only 150 males and 30 females remain alive. It's clear that large-beaked birds have survived in greater numbers than small-beaked birds.

More males have also survived. Because of their slightly larger bodies and beaks, they are better able to crack the more plentiful, larger seeds.

MATING

I learned that number 1362 picked one of the older males as her mate. How can we tell he's older?

All finches are brown and streaked when young. Females keep this color, but males become blacker and blacker as they shed and regrow their feathers. With the first shed (or molt), their head feathers grow in black. After several molts all their feathers are black.

The finches' courtship is captivating. Each male builds several display nests. These are usually not used for eggs. They seem to be just for show for the ladies.

Imagine male humans building several homes so the female humans can inspect them!

The drought lasted eighteen months — three times longer than the normal dry season. Then came the rain, and plenty of it. Within a week of the downpours, the plants had already sprouted leaves. Caterpillars crawled over the new flower buds. Male birds sang.

Adelita flew into several males' territories, one after another. During her visit to the third territory, a male with shiny, black feathers and a big beak landed right in front of her. She inspected the condition of his feathers and his coloring. He moved his wings back and forth so quickly they seemed to vibrate.

Is he trying to impress me?

She flew over to examine the part of the island he had claimed to see if he would be a good provider.

Is there plenty of food? Yes!

Is the nest secure and safe from interference from predators and other birds? Yes!

Adelita chose him as her mate. Perhaps she would spend the rest of her life with this bird.

Scratch, scratch, scratch.

Adelita peeked into the side entrance of the nest. She cocked her head at the scraping sounds coming from four, white, speckled eggs. Much later that day a tiny hole appeared in one.

Eventually the first chick, wet and gooey, emerged from its shell. It had huge eyes, an oversized beak, and tiny wings.

I'm a mother!

Plop. It fell over. The hatchling scrambled to right itself and opened its beak wide. Adelita moved to action. Off she flew in search of food.

Ah, a fat juicy caterpillar. Perfect.

The new mother and her mate spent the next month finding food and feeding seeds, insects, and pollen to their young, just as her parents had done for her.

A DISCOVERY

Peter and Rosemary have just sent intriguing news about their recent measurements on Daphne Major Island. They have determined that the average bill size of the finches is now four-to-five percent bigger than it was for the population of birds alive before the drought. This large-bill trait has become more common in the population in a very short time — two years!

Larger-beaked birds survived the drought in greater numbers. That explains why the average bill size is larger in part, but it's not just that. It's also because of the way the females chose mates: there were many more males than females after the drought, and each female had her pick of mates — some males weren't picked at all. And guess what? The males with larger bills got chosen. The females picked males with larger beaks after the drought and the chicks inherited larger beaks. The Grants documented this finch discovery.

RETURN TRIP FOUR YEARS LATER

The rain! It brought on such plant growth. We could almost see the grasses shooting up and the vines becoming thicker and more tangled. El Niño, an unusually warm ocean current off Peru and Ecuador, was the cause. This year El Niño felt much warmer than anyone could remember. Because it was warmer, more water evaporated from the ocean and it then returned to earth as rain.

The caltrop plants were totally overcome by vines, and the cactuses didn't produce fruit because the ground was too wet. We rarely found large seeds. This weather had the opposite effect of the drought. Vines and grasses created a bounty of small seeds. Our plots contained twelve times the amount of seeds available in a normal year. They were mostly small, soft seeds.

During each of the next four wet seasons, Adelita and her mate spent many hours caring for their young. Luckily, several years of long wet seasons followed and seeds of all sizes were plentiful.

When Adelita was eight, the weather changed again. Rain fell for days and days. The plants that produced large seeds did not flower, but the plants that produced small seeds grew fast, multiplied, and covered the ground.

Little seeds and caterpillars were everywhere, and Adelita and her mate raised eight sets of chicks in eight months. Other finches did as well. The island became a bustling home for chirping chicks.

CHICKS EVERYWHERE

During the long drought, less than an inch (24 mm) of rain fell. In the nine months of the severe El Niño season, four and a half feet (1.359 m) of rain poured out of the sky! No wonder the plants grew so much. And the babies! After the drought, we had counted only 180 small-beaked survivors. Then, after the extra-long rainy season caused by El Niño, we counted 1,000. The breeding season ends when the rainy season stops — so the extra-long rainy season meant an extra-long breeding season. Even some three-month-old birds mated! Normally, finches don't mate until they are two years old.

But with the drought that followed and the deaths of many large beaked birds, we took measurements again and noted that the finches' average bill size was smaller.

The small bill trait is now more common in the population!

A drought returned the next year when Adelita was nine. Her mate's bigger body needed more food than hers, but there were few large seeds and few insects now, and his big beak could not grasp and crack the small seeds very well. Adelita's mate became weak with hunger. He barely moved. Soon her first mate closed his eyes. He had starved to death.

Adelita needed to find another mate. She flew in and out of several males' territories. Each was singing from the tallest cactus in his area.

There were lots of males with small beaks, but fewer of the large-beaked males had survived.

As she was inspecting one nest, a small-beaked male flew toward her, singing, swaying from side to side, and fluttering from perch to perch.

After inspecting his territory, Adelita chose him as her new mate. Soon they were busy parents feeding their new young.

A new dry season had begun. Adelita perched on a branch and surveyed her territory. She knew this part of the island well.

She had lived through years that were unusually wet and years that were unusually dry, surviving the natural cycles of the island. This was part of life for Adelita.

Two of the humans came near. They looked at her. She turned to look at them.

Perhaps she'd fly off to get food or perhaps she'd fly over and land on one of their heads!

A REMARKABLE STUDY

Peter and Rosemary's dedicated work has made scientific history. After the severe drought, the generations of finches that followed had mostly bigger beaks. Then after the abundant rains again changed the food supply on their island, the next generations tended to have smaller beaks. Their study measured microevolution in action. What's microevolution? It is a change in the frequency of a gene in a population. The Grants saw it happen twice in just eleven years! They also saw the finches adopt new behaviors when needed.

Are there lessons for humans in this extraordinary study? How can we adapt to our changing world? What new ideas do we need to implement? Can we select the best of them and run with what works?

As for more research, where will I go next?

Perhaps to be with scientists who study marmots, or polar bears, or mosquitoes? I wonder how they adapt?

Timeline

The Grants arrive on Daphne Major Island, in 1973, during the wet season.

The Grants return in August 1973, during the dry season.

A severe drought occurs from June 1977 to January 1978.

A severe El Niño event produces eight months of rain from November 1982 to July 1983.

Acknowledgments

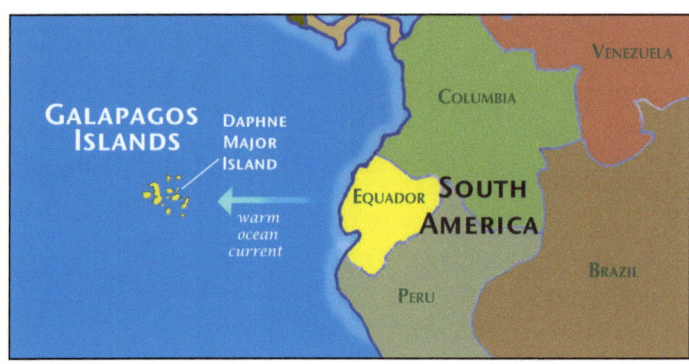

I've written here about Peter and Rosemary Grant, yet other scientists helped with this research. In 1973 the Grants' arrived with their daughters Nicola and Thalia (then age 8 and 6), along with Ian and Lynette Abbott. Peter Boag, Lisle Gibbs, Trevor Price, Laurene Ratcliffe, Dolph Schluter, Jamie Smith, and Ayse Unal also participated in the research during this period in the 70s and 80s.

Amazingly enough, the work on finches in the Galapagos continues to this day with many other scientists participating.

My sincere thanks to Rosemary and Peter Grant, Professors Emeriti at Princeton University, for their review and suggestions.

Helpful resources included *The Beak of the Finch* by Jonathan Weiner and books and articles written by Peter and Rosemary Grant.

In 2002, the Dresden School District in Hanover, New Hampshire, provided a curriculum grant allowing me to participate in an eleven-day, natural history tour in the Galapagos Islands. Peter and Rosemary's son-in-law, biologist Greg Estes, and naturalist Martin Loyola were our instructors. I am deeply grateful for that incredible learning opportunity.

Feedback from Pomfret Elementary School students in Pomfret, Vermont, and from the elementary and middle school students in Hanover was quite instructive. Len Reitsma, professor and avian ecologist at Plymouth State University, Dr. John Lloyd, senior scientist at the Ecostudies Institute, and Tom Sherry, professor of bird population ecology and conservation biology at Tulane University, helped with accuracy.

It was a delight to work with Bert Dodson, the illustrator. Thank you, Bert, for your patience, dedication, humor, love of science, and great skill as an artist!

Thank you, Jenna Dixon, for your creativity, sense of play, wit, and book design.

Friends, colleagues, and professional editor Joni Cole were writing coaches, editors, and support.

I particularly thank Judy Pond, Jody Horan, Joan Waltermire, Jim McCracken, Anne Hansen, Bill Weiler, Cynthia Taylor, Mary Bryant, Denise Reitsma, Tii McLane, Marge Dedell, and my mom, Doris Wallis.

Thank you, all!